RAILS AROUND

READING

in COLOR

by

Benjamin L. Bernhart

featuring photographs from

**Bruce Adams, Craig Bossler, Jim Bross, Paul Carpenito,
William C. Cauff, Jr., George Washington Gerhart,
Robert Gottschall, Jr., Jay Leinbach, Sam Lenhart,
Outer Station Project, John Stoudt, Jr., Robert Wanner,
and the Reading Transportation Museum**

edited by

**Jay Leinbach, Melissa D. Bernhart,
and Dr. John H. L. Bernhart**

Along the Historic Reading Main Line

Celebrating 175 Years of Reading Railroad History 1833-2008

In Memory of
George Hart
February 12, 1919 - April 17, 2008

A Man Who Devoted His Life To Preserving Railroad History!

George Hart heading out on a rail fan excursion in his 1931 Plymouth.
Photographed by Sam Lenhart in 1972.

Current Titles by the Outer Station Project

***Central Railroad of New Jersey
Stations, Structures and
Marine Equipment***
$29.95

Reading - Jersey Central Magazines
Book 1 Vol. 1, Issues 1-6
Book 2 Vol. 1, Issues 7-12
$60.00 for Set

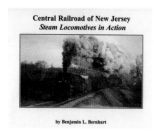

***Central Railroad of New Jersey
Steam Locomotives in Action***
$12.00

***The Reading Railroad's
Mighty Pacifics***
$39.95

Shortlines & Industrial Railroads of New Jersey
From the Camera & Collection of Thurlow C. Haunton, Jr.
Volume 1 $24.95, Volume 2 $24.95
Limited Edition Hard Cover $60.00

Hoboken Shore Railroad
$10.00

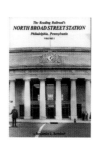

***The Reading Railroad's
North Broad Street Station***
$10.00

New York & Long Branch
A Photographic Remembrance with John Truitt
$17.95

The Derailment of the Congressional Limited
Pennsylvania's Worst Railroad Disaster
$12.00

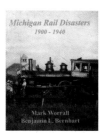

***Michigan Rail Disasters
1900-1940***
Soft Cover $34.95
LE Hard Cover $60.00

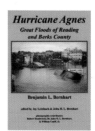

Hurricane Agnes
Great Floods of Reading and Berks County
$20.00

Outer Station Project Publications

Outer Station Project

1335 Railroad Road, Dauberville, PA 19533

(610) 916-2433   OSPpublications@aol.com

Many other transportation titles available
from numerous large and small publishers.
Please call for a catalogue.

READING RAILROAD
MAGAZINE

VOLUME 25   ISSUE 1
JANUARY, 2009

252

Preserving
Reading Railroad
Heritage
Since 1899

Feature Articles
Reading Railroad Logos
Reading Transportation Museum

AFTER 28 YEARS - - IT'S BACK ON TRACK!

STEAMING TO YOU

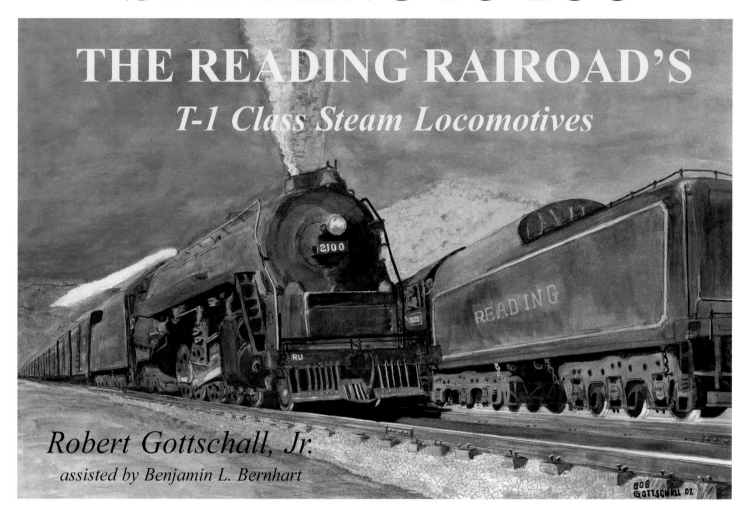

THE READING RAIROAD'S

T-1 Class Steam Locomotives

Robert Gottschall, Jr.
assisted by Benjamin L. Bernhart

IN OCTOBER, 2008

**Written from original records housed in the Reading Transportation Museum.
Relates the T-1 Story from conception to the last revenue freight run.
A Ground Breaking Documentary.**

Reading
Transportation
Museum

Published by the

**Reading Transportation Museum,
P.O. Box 15211, Reading, PA 19612**

www.ReadingTransportationMuseum.org

Author's Preface

My father had the privilege of growing up in the city of Reading when steam locomotives still roamed the rails. As he matured from child to adult, so did the motive power of the Reading Railroad. From his home on Green Street he could look down the hill onto the Outer Station complex. Spending many days standing on the Swinging Bridge, he watched the *Mighty Pacifics* and the *T-1s* be replaced by the ALCO RS3s, the FP7s and other first generation diesels. His favorites were the powerful Fairbanks Morse Trainmasters. It was from his daily commute to college that he watched the beginning of the second generation diesel locomotives come to dominance.

Living history is what my father, Dr. John H. L. Bernhart, was doing. He recorded these events in his mind and to this day can recall many of the exact dates and times of these experiences. Countless family photographs were taken, but it never occurred to him to capture the railroad on film. The railroad had always been there; he could not image how quickly it would disappear, or that it would be important to preserve it on film. Therefore, while the railroad was transforming before his eyes, less than two dozen photographs of that transformation can be accredited to his own shutter. An amateur rail fan is how my father would describe himself.

As a serious railroad historian you would think that I myself would take numerous railroad photographs; however, this is not the case. Although not as dramatic, I too have watched a transformation of rail service in Berks County. I saw the Reading Railroad become part of Conrail, the rise of the Reading & Northern and the demise of Conrail as it became part of Norfolk Southern and CSX. Yet, like my father I have taken very few photographs. Modern railroading just is not as much "*fun*" as trying to relive the Reading Railroad.

Two of the photographs the author's father, Dr. John H.L. Bernhart took of the Reading Railroad. The top image depicts the Push-Pull train arriving at the Franklin Street Station on August 15, 1972. The author's older brother and sister have just deboarded an RDC at Franklin Street Station on January 1, 1972. During the trip from Hamburg, the conductor proudly announced to the passengers that it was the 130th anniversary of the first run on the completed Pottsville - Philadelphia Main Line!

Fortunately there were several individuals who did capture, on film, the transformation on rails in Berks County between 1950 and 1976 and their works or collected images are displayed throughout this book. I must thank Bruce Adams, Jim Bross, Paul Carpenito, William C. Cauff, Jr., Robert Gottschall, Jr., Jay Leinbach, Sam Lenhart, Robert Wanner, John Stoudt, Jr., Andrew Porambo, James Brownback, and George Washington Gerhart for allowing their photographs to be shared with all.

This book was produced purely for the enjoyment of viewing images of the Reading Railroad, the Pennsylvania Railroad, the Penn Central Railroad, and the Reading Street Railway in the areas around the city of Reading and Berks County. Although some historical and technical information is provided, this publication is not meant to be a comprehensive study of this area. So sit back and enjoy this pictorial tour of "Rails Around Reading."

About the Author

Benjamin L. Bernhart first became interested in railroads as he was growing up along the abandoned Schuylkill & Lehigh Branch of the Reading Company. His interest was further fostered during the Bernhart family trips to visit relatives within the city of Reading, Pennsylvania. A drive along Sixth Street, paralleling the Reading Railroad shops, was a routine event. At the young age of fourteen, Mr. Bernhart began his railroad career as a volunteer on the Wanamaker, Kempton & Southern Railroad.

As a teenager Benjamin L. Bernhart moved to the city of Reading, graduating from Reading High School in 1991. During his high school senior year, Benjamin wrote his first publication entitled *The Outer Station, Reading, Pennsylvania.* In 1993, he was awarded a prestigious research fellowship from the Hagley Museum & Library, spending a summer researching the letter books of G.A. Nicolls, the first general superintendent of the Philadelphia & Reading Railroad. Mr. Bernhart attended Albright College and graduated from its Honors Program with a BA in History. Serving as an historical consultant, Mr. Bernhart has been employed by the City of Reading and the Lancaster County Planning Commissions to conduct historical research into rail transportation within those governmental jurisdictions.

Upon graduation Benjamin Bernhart followed his career dream by obtaining a position with the Pennsylvania Historic Museum Commission at the Railroad Museum of Pennsylvania. During this time, he was also employed by the Strasburg Rail Road. Due to family commitments, Mr. Bernhart returned to the city of Reading in 1997 and continued to author publications, receiving in 1999 the "Outstanding Citizenship Award" from the Mayor of Reading for his work in preserving the heritage of the city. In 1990 Mr. Bernhart was also honored with the title "Reading Company Historian" by Reading Company president, James Wunderly.

Benjamin L. Bernhart currently sits on the Board of Trustees of the Historical Society of Berks County and was the guest curator for their major exhibit honoring the Reading Railroad's 175th anniversary in 2008. Mr. Bernhart also serves as curator for the Reading Transportation Museum. He is also a member of the Friends of the Railroad Museum of Pennsylvania, the Pennsylvania Railroad Technical & Historical Society and the Train Collectors Association. Mr. Bernhart has written over thirty publications and numerous articles. He currently works as an independent historian, with his office located along the historic Main Line of the Reading Railroad. For information on hiring Mr. Bernhart, please write to him at: 1335 Railroad Road, Dauberville, PA 19533, call him at (610) 916-2433 or email him at OSPpublications@aol.com.

Want To Get Published?

The Outer Station Project is a full service publishing firm which offers authors or photographers a chance to get their works published. We help authors or photographers get started and guide them through the complex world of printing, distribution and marketing. The Outer Station Project is currently looking for authors or photographers for future publications. Best of all, you keep the copyright to your works. The Outer Station Project has access to the latest digital technology and can transform your photograph collection onto a digital media.

Top: With FP-7 A unit 903 at the point, an eastbound "Push-Pull" passenger train glides through Douglassville, circa 1976. The Reading Company Station was located to the right of the track. At this point the Reading and the Pennsylvania Railroad tracks were side by side. The Pennsylvania Railroad tracks and their Douglasville Station can be seen to the left of the train. The PRR two story combination station was built in 1884. A short distance beyond the station the Pennsylvania Railroad crossed the Schuylkill River and traveled on the west bank to the city of Reading while the Reading traveled on the east bank. **Bottom:** The first of 20 GP39-2 diesel locomotives arrived on the Reading in November, 1974. Diesel 3401 and two unidentified units pull a short consist towards Pottstown in 1975. Both photographs Jay Leinbach.

BIRDSBORO

Page 10 - Top: Robert Gottschall, Jr. took this "winter postcard" of a westbound passenger train on December 24, 1969. The four Budd built RDCs are slowing to make a station stop at the 1887 Frank Furness influnced Birdsboro Station. **Bottom:** An eastbound passenger train is stopped at the Birdsboro Station in October, 1962. The Fairbanks Morse Trainmaster diesel locomotives were workhorses and were often used in both passenger and freight service. Collection of the Outer Station Project.

Top: Three Budd RDCs make up this May 27, 1976, westbound passenger train. RDG Transportation Museum. **Middle:** The E&G Brooke Plant (the Wickwire Spencer Steel Division of the Colorado Fuel & Iron Corporation) was located just north of the Birdsboro Station. This saddle tank engine was sold to the WK&S Railroad, where its sits at Kempton on August 13, 1969. Outer Station Project. **Bottom:** On May 7, 1961, T-1 2124 pulls an "Iron Horse Rail Ramble" past the Birdsboro Station. The E&G Brooke Plant is in the background. James D. Brownback.

Top: Just north of the Birdsboro Station two RDCs head southward in April, 1975. Their destination is the Reading Terminal, Philadelphia. The author remembers taking these RDC passenger trains to Philadelphia every Christmas season to shop at John Wanamaker's, located across from the Reading Terminal. Inside the flagship store was a multi-story light pageant which retold several popular Christmas stories -- and who could forget the monorail which ran around the ceiling of the toy department? Jay Leinbach.

Middle: Coming off the Reading Belt Line and onto the Main Line, a freight train being pulled by GP35 diesels 3642, 3647 and 3632 passes the Birdsboro Station. RDG Transportation Museum.

Bottom: Two GP39-2 diesel locomotives, units 3410 and 3416, pull a string of empty hopper cars northward toward the anthracite coal region. Jay Leinbach.

Page 13: Two views of FP7 A-unit 900 providing the motive power for the westbound "Push-Pull" as it rounds the curve at Birdsboro Station. The idea for the "Push-Pull" train was generated after a very crowded and over capacity RDC passenger train bottomed out, damaging a switch frog as it rounded Klapperthal Curve. Top photograph circa 1976 by Sam Lenhart. Bottom photograph April, 1976 by Jay Leinbach.

Top: The Reading Company maintained a freight house in downtown Birdsboro along the Wilmington & Northern Branch. The frame structure was built in 1885. The freight house can be seen behind the SW900m diesel locomotive. One wonders why the word "MOUSE" is inscribed upon the engine, possibly a joke among crew members or an unofficial name for the diesel. The locomotive arrived on the Reading in 1941 as a Baldwin VO660 switcher. Twenty years later it was rebuilt into the EMD SW switcher this picture depicts. It appears the unit was recently repainted in this August, 1975 view. Jay Leinbach Collection.

Bottom: The Reading Belt Line terminated at Birdsboro. Caboose 94116 makes up the rear of an eastbound freight train as it enters Birdsboro and crosses the Schuylkill River to travel down the Main Line. Reading Transportation Museum.

LORAINE - EXETER

Top: Three Rail Diesel Cars (RDC) make up this June, 1975, westbound passenger train as it passes the Bully Lyons Hotel. Reading Transportation Museum.

Bottom: In June, 1975, the "Push-Pull" train passes through Exeter Township on its way to Reading. The train is No. 7. Reading Transportation Museum.

NEVERSINK

Page 16: By the time these three photographs of Reading Company trains passing Neversink were taken, the former flag stop station had long since been removed. The top image depicts GP30 3617 pulling a westbound freight, circa 1975. A lone RDC making its way to Philadelphia during an evening in 1976 is shown in the middle. The bottom photograph captures diesel 3605 heading eastbound with a long string of freight cars in October, 1975. All photographs Jay Leinbach.

Top: On September 3, 1960, an Iron Horse Rail Ramble rounds Klapperthal Curve on its way back to Reading as it passes eastbound passenger train No. 1008. The excursion left the Outer Station at 10:00 AM, traveled along the East Penn Branch, down the Perkiomen Branch, and returned to Reading via the Main Line. After the eastbound passenger train passed, passengers debarked the train for a "speed" picture stop. The cost for an adult ticket was

$5.00, or a mere $40.00 in 2007 dollars. Where in the United States can you get a steam excursion of this caliber for that low price? The Reading Company sure knew how put on a show! Bruce Adams. **Bottom:** This unusual backup move of FT 252 A&B was made at Klapperthal Junction in order to deliver and shift coal cars at the Titus Power Plant. These two diesel units were not connected by a standard coupler but by a drawbar. Therefore the unit was considered to be one 2,700 horsepower locomotive. Jay Leinbach collection.

Page 18: Klapperthal Junction as seen from on top of the Neversink Mountain. Train No. 2008 passes through the interlocking on May 29, 1953. Note the undeveloped valley and the South 9th Street Bridge over the railroad in the upper right corner. **Page 19:** Train No. 7 rounds the curve just north of Klapperthal and will soon pass under the South 9th Street Bridge, circa 1953. Both photographs Robert Wanner.

Page 20: Two of the City of Reading's icons, the Reading Brewing Company and the Pagoda, which overlooks the city on Mt. Penn, appear in these two photographs of train No. 7 arriving in Reading from the south in March, 1975. The lone man walking his dog was a Reading Company police officer who was nicknamed "Dick Tracy" by railfans for his uncanny ability to know when and where someone was on company property without permission. Both Photographs Reading Transportation Museum.

Top: The "Push-Pull" train passes the original Reading Railroad locomotive shops at 7th & Chestnut Streets upon its arrival at the Franklin Street Station. Sam Lenhart. **Middle:** The circumstances under which the "Push-Pull" train is meeting a Pottsville-Reading RDC and a Reading-Philadelphia RDC at the Franklin Street Station are unknown. A three train meet at the station was not an everyday occurrence. Sam Lenhart. **Bottom:** The Station as it appeared in 1976. The P&R Loco Shop is in the background. Jay Leinbach.

FRANKLIN STREET

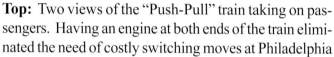

Top: Two views of the "Push-Pull" train taking on passengers. Having an engine at both ends of the train eliminated the need of costly switching moves at Philadelphia or Reading. Jay Leinbach. **Bottom:** This circa 1955 photograph depicts FP7 901 and one of its sisters coupled back to back. Together they will pull the train northward to Pottsville. At Pottsville the coaches would be pulled away from the diesels. The engines would then move on to a side track while the coaches were being placed back under the trainshed. The diesels then recoupled on the southern end of the coaches for the return trip. This move was not only time consuming but also required the wages of an additional crew. The "Push-Pull" arrangement eliminated this extra costly move. Jay Leinbach Collection.

Top: In 1965 the railroad realized they needed additional RDCs and purchased two from the Boston & Maine Railroad. Ex-B&M 6205 became RDG 9165. The Reading converted the baggage compartment into a snack bar and dubbed it the "Refreshment Car." RDC 9165 sits at Franklin Street station in March, 1976. **Middle:** During the presidental years of E.P. Gangware passenger train neglect was a common occurence. The color of this photograph is not incorrect, the RDC is just that filthy! Reading Transportation Mueseum.

Bottom: The Reading Company ran several railfan excusions properly named "Fairwell To The Reading" in March, 1976. These trips were the railfan's last opportunity to enjoy rail rambles under the Reading herald and therefore were well patronized and photographed. At 9:30 AM on March 21, 1976, the consist for that day's trip crosses over Cherry Street on its way to pickup passengers at the Franklin Street Station. Reading Transportation Museum.

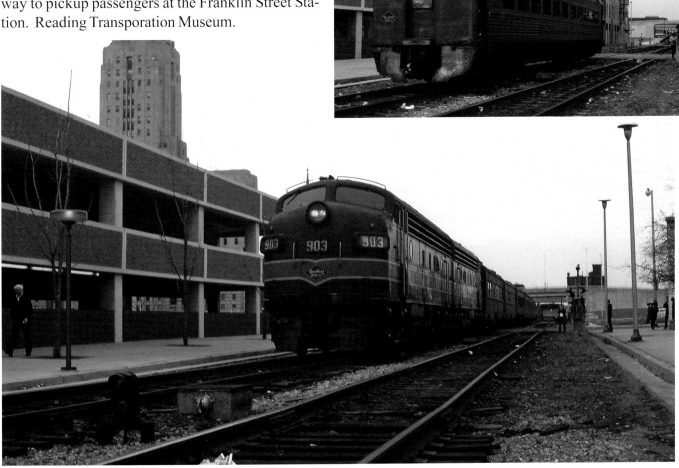

Page 24: Passengers from Philadelphia and points south of Reading arrived on a pair of RDCs, one of them being RDC 9166, an ex-B&M RR RDC. Passengers bound for points north of Reading and Pottsville boarded the lone RDC. The pair of RDCs from Philadelphia are in the process of traveling to a siding at the Outer Station where they will layover until their return trip to Philadelphia. A westbound RDC is passing the pair of RDCs on the eastbound track. It will switch over to the westbound track inside the infamous 7th Street Cut. Paul Carpenito.

7th STREET CUT

Top: From Penn Street to Walnut Street, the Reading Railroad traveled through a narrow cut in the landscape known as the 7th Street Cut. In 1877 this narrow stretch of ground became the site of the bloodest massacre in the history of the city of Reading. Railroad employees were on strike and assembled inside the cut, effectively stopping train movements. The Pennsylvania State Militia was called to the site to restore order. Gunfire broke out and ten people were killed and twice as many were injuried.

Three streets originally crossed this cut using simple wooden truss bridges. In March, 1970, Reading Company engineers, along with officials from the city and Berks County, met at the wooden Court Street bridge to discuss its replacement. The gentleman wearing a hardhat is one of those officials. William C. Cauff, Jr.

Bottom: Appearently the Reading Company was not too superstitious for the last of the first group of seven EMD GP7 diesel locomotives, which arrived on the railroad in 1952, was numbered 666. A pair of GP7 diesels pull the "Schuylkill" through the 7th Street Cut on May 1, 1955. Collection Jay Leinbach.

Top Left: The crossover inside the 7ᵗʰ Street Cut. Today only one track travels through the cut.
Top Right: The 1866 Walnut Street Bridge in August, 1970. Renowned author John Updike added to the historical lore of the cut and the Walnut Street Bridge when he wrote about them in "Rabbit Run" and in "Rabbit at Rest."

. . .in a wooden-railed hump to pass over, the laborers of old hand-dug a great trench to bring the railroad tracks into the city, tracks disused now, and the cut, walled in limestone, a pit for tossing beer cans and soda bottles down into, whole garbage bags even, mattresses. (Updike, "Rabbit at Rest").

Bottom: The city's ill-fated attempt to revitalize downtown Reading had already begun when Paul Carpenito captured the railroad's train known as the "Joanna Turn" crossing Penn Street in August, 1974.

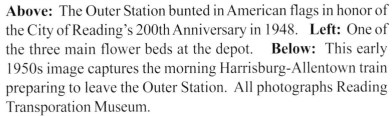

Above: The Outer Station bunted in American flags in honor of the City of Reading's 200th Anniversary in 1948. **Left:** One of the three main flower beds at the depot. **Below:** This early 1950s image captures the morning Harrisburg-Allentown train preparing to leave the Outer Station. All photographs Reading Transporation Museum.

Top: A pair of ALCO RS-3 diesel locomotives pull into Platform 1 underneath the Main Line train shed at the Outer Station, circa 1953. The train has arrived from Philadelphia and will continue its journey up the Main Line. Reading Transportation Museum.

Middle: During the "Glory Years" of railroading there were several special trains that criss-crossed America to promote different industries and advacements in progress of humanity. Sometime during 1953 or 1954 the "Schoolroom Progress U.S.A." train stopped at the Outer Station for public inspection. Reading Transportation Museum.

Bottom: Two GP7 diesel locomotives arrive at the Outer Station with a westbound train. Collection Jay Leinbach.   **Page 29:** Central Railroad of New Jersey GP7 1524 pulls train No. 193, the "Harrisburg Special," out of the Lebanon Valley train shed on April 2, 1953. The train originated at Jersey City, New Jersey and will terminate in Harrisburg, Pennsylvania. Robert Wanner.

Top: The Outer Station complex as it appeared on May 2, 1964. RDG Transportation Museum. Middle: Just three short years after this 1963 photograph of the Outer Station was taken the Reading Railroad began removing departments and their offices from the building. The railroad had already drastically cut back their maintance on the building and grounds. The seasonal "Reading Lines" flower garden had been discontinued. RDG Transportation Museum. Bottom Left: Jay Leinbach took this view of the Outer Station complex from his 4th floor apartment at 5th & Greenwich Streets, circa 1975. Bottom Right: The Outer Station's Main Line (front) doors. The white sheets of paper hanging on the doors tell passengers that on March 9, 1969, passenger trains will no longer stop at the station. RDG Transportation Museum.

Top: The Swinging Bridge became a symbol of the Reading Railroad. On August 4, 1887, several hundred members of St. John's Lutheran Church crossed the foot bridge that was designed and built by the John A. Roebling's Sons Company. Their unison step made the bridge sway, making it impossible to cross. Since that day, until it was closed to pedestrians in May, 1967, the swaying of the bridge awed thousands! Originally the bridge was painted a light orange with blue and grey cables -- a sight to behold! Reading Transportation Museum. **Bottom:** The commodious 8th Street Freight House was located across from the Outer Station. William C. Cauff, Jr.

Page 32: The Outer Station was a social, economic, and spiritual center for not only Reading Railroad employees but for the citizens of Reading and Berks County. It is one of the few locations that is remembered by the majority of Berks Countians and visiting travelers from near and far! One reason for this phenomenon was that railroad employees made the station complex feel special. Decorating the station for the holidays is just one example. Railroad official Andrew J. Porambo took these rare images of the 1957 and 1958 Christmas displays that greeted all on the 6th Street lawn and inside the Outer Station. Reading Transportation Museum.

Top: On May 6, 1973, the conductor watches his train move past the Outer Station with FP7s 902 and 900 providing the motive power. Ludens Candy is the large building in the background. Reading Transportation Museum. **Middle Left:** The coaches of the "Push-Pull" train sit at the Outer Station in March, 1969. Note the double crossover switch. Reading Transportation Museum. **Middle Right:** FP7 900 at Reading. William C. Cauff, Jr. **Bottom:** The first Reading Company RDC to roam the railroad's rails was RDC 9153 in November, 1962. In March, 1969, RDC 9153 makes one of its last stops at the Outer Station before the station stop was discontinued. Reading Transportation Museum.

Top: On September 27, 1966, GP30 3601 rounds the curve at the Outer Station and will soon travel underneath the bridge carrying 5th Street over the railroad tracks. The train is bound for Rutherford along the Lebanon Valley Branch. Reading Transportation Museum. **Middle:** The yard was a busy place as demonstrated by the number of rolling stock which appears between the freight house and the Outer Station. Jay Leinbach Collection. **Bottom:** Bringing our exploration of the Outer Station to a close is caboose 92866 passing Oley Tower in March, 1971. Reading Transportation Museum.

Top: A Baldwin model DS-4-4-1000 switching locomotive sits in front of Oley Tower and is being inspected by several rail fans. Jay Leinbach Collection.   **Bottom:** Diesel 2757, an SW1500, pulls a draft of freight cars past Oley Tower. Oley Tower still stands today and is used by Norfolk Southern. Reading Transportation Museum.

Top: Directly behind diesel 1503 is the Reading Company's store house. In the early 1990s the building was renovated into a retail mall called "Reading Station Outlet." The mall only survived a few years before closing. Today the majority of the building sits vacant. Reading Transportation Museum.

Middle: SW900m 1504 pulls a box car past the Spring Street Yard Office on June 15, 1975. The yard office was a very busy place. The office served as the central operating point of the yard and through its doors was a constant flow of through crews, shifting crews, and car inspectors. Jay Leinbach Collection. **Bottom:** On September 9, 1972, several mighty diesels sit in front of the Spring Street Yard Office, awaiting their next assignment. Reading Transportation Museum.

Top: To meet the overwhelming demand, the Reading Railroad ran another Iron Horse Ramble to West Milton on October 19, 1963. Two trains meet at Reading, one from Philadelphia and one from Harrisburg, both of which were pulled by one of the famous T-1 class steam locomotives. Certain sections of the trip were powered by diesel locomotives. Three diesel units, one of which is FP7 906, combine the two sections at Reading. Smoke from the steam locomotives can be seen at the rear of the train. With both T-1 steam locomotives at the point the combined ramble left Reading at 8:45 AM. **Bottom:** Nine years later two FP7 diesels pull a National Railroad Historical Society special past the same spot as the above image. Both photographs Reading Transportation Museum.

Top: It's the first day of Conrail, April 1, 1976, but for now the status quo continues. RDC 9159, now considered to be ex-Reading, makes a scheduled stop at the Spring Street Yard Office to pickup railroad employees who commuted by rail. **Middle & Bottom:** Two views of equipment stored at Reading during January & February, 1976. Reading Transportation Museum.

Top: This March 10, 1974, view of diesel locomotives depicts just a small sample of the many different classes of motive power which could be found inside the Reading Yards. Shown from left to right are: ALCO RS3 503, an unidentified ALCO C630, EMD SW1500 2751, and ALCO RS3 465. **Bottom:** GP30 3600 sits at the southern end of the Locomotive Shops in December, 1972. Both photographs Reading Transportation Museum.

Top: Access into the Reading Yards by rail fans was difficult. Many photographs were taken from the public sidewalk that parallels the yard along North 6th Street, such as this image taken with a telephoto lens in November, 1974. Behind SW1 21 and the two tank cars are the noses of two ALCO RS3 diesel locomotives. The Great Northern RDC was rehabilitated and relettered by Reading Railroad employees for use by Amtrak. Paul Carpenito.
Bottom: RS3 465 is working the yard at Spring Street on January 30, 1974. This unit was the last of the ALCO RS3s in operation on the Reading Railroad. Reading Transportation Museum.

Top: FT 251 A&B units along side the Reading Locomotive Shops. This diesel pair was built by EMD during January, 1945, and was first placed in service on February 5, 1945. In 1962 the two diesel units were traded in for credit on GP30 5511 and 5512. Jay Leinbach Collection.

Middle: Behind Reading switcher 716 is a Western Maryland Railroad diesel. When this image was taken in September, 1972, it was not uncommon to see foreign motive power in the Reading Yards. Reading Transportation Museum.

Bottom: SW1500 diesel 2757, Reading Railroad class SWE-14, eases into the Reading Locomotive Shop sometime during the first week of Conrail, April, 1976. Reading Transportation Museum.

Pages 42 & 43: Four views of the Reading Locomotive Shops steam locomotive -- small but powerful enough to move large engines around the shop complex. By the time these May 29, 1954, images were taken, diesel locomotives had already proven their dominance. Two large T-1 steam locomotives sit in reserve between the turntable and the coaling tower. Reading Transportation Museum.

Top: A Conrail employee climbs onto ex-Reading SW1500 2767 to assist in shifting freight cars around the yard during a hot July, 1976 evening. Conrail has been in operation for several months, but this unit still displays its Reading heritage and number. The diesel will soon be painted blue and renumbered to 9617. Reading Transportation Museum.

Middle & Bottom: Two views of GP7 625 at work at the northern end of the yard at a location known as "Water" on February 24, 1974. Water was a brick tower structure located just north of the Richmond Street / Heister's Lane culvert. The diesel is working what was known as the "Ram." Performing the "Ram" meant you were sorting, shifting, and putting together the countless freight trains that left the yards. Reading Transportation Museum.

Top: In February, 1974, a freight train being hauled by GP40-2 3673 & 3675 arrives at Reading. The large, imposing castle on the hill is the Reading High School. At one time the high school sponsored a railroad club for its students and had a friendly relationship with the Reading Railroad. **Bottom:** Diesels 3242, 5201 & 3672 leave the Reading Yards with a long string of freight cars. Both photographs Reading Transportation Museum.

Top: Shifting cars at Water is MP15 2776 in July, 1976. RDG Transportation Museum.

Middle: ALCO C-630 5310, a RSA-14 class, glides northward out of the Reading Yards with a freight train in May, 1975. RDG Transportation Museum.

Bottom: Action at Water! Smoke rises from an ALCO RS3 as it performs the Ram duties while a freight arrives in March, 1974. Reading Transportation Museum.

Top: Six diesel locomotives, possibly some of them in tow, head up this freight train as it travels out of the northern section of the Reading Yards. Judging from the shadows and the sun glare on the diesels, evening is upon us on March 6, 1976. The diesel units that can be identified are two MP15 units, 2777 & 2779, and GP40-2 3672.
Bottom: State of Maine Products box cars were once a common sight on northeastern railroads. During potato season these box cars transported thousands of bushels of potatoes from the Pine Tree State. During the off season they were leased to other industries. Note the State of Maine Products box car behind GP35s 3652 & 3654 as they head out of the Reading Yard in August, 1974. Both photographs Reading Transportation Museum.

Top: Leaving Reading with the Newberry run are diesels 3652, 7602 and 3653 during a mid-afternoon in February, 1974. **Bottom:** The crew of GP35 3623 waits for clearance as SD45 7602 and GP30 3617 head toward Belt Line Junction on a wintery day in March, 1972. Both photographs Reading Transportation Museum.

Top: City officials would not allow the Reading Railroad to construct a fueling station within the Reading Yards. Therefore, the fueling facility was located just over the city's border in Muhlenburg Township. This illustration shows the fueling facility as it appeared from on top of one the fuel storage tanks. The Reading Yards can be seen in the upper right corner. William C. Cauff, Jr. Collection.

Middle: The "DF" on box car 18721 stands for "Delicate Freight." The railroad and all of its employees took pride in preventing damage to goods during transit. At one time the railroad even constructed a special box car, with chicken wire for side sheeting, to illustrate how improperly loaded freight shifts, resulting in damage **Bottom:** RDC 9152 passes GP7 625 working the Ram in front of the scale house on February 24, 1974. Both photographs Reading Transportation Museum.

Top: In October, 1975, diesels 3416 and 3415, a pair of GP39-2, have just finished speeding around the city of Reading on the Belt Line. This priority trailer train is crossing Route 61 and will travel through the interlocking at Belt Line Junction on its journey eastward. Jay Leinbach Collection.   **Bottom:** FT 250 A&B at Belt Line Junction on June 18, 1960. The train is bound for the Reading Yards. Jay Leinbach Collection.

Page 51: Two different views of a Pottsville - Reading RDC train passing Belt Line Junction during the fall of 1975. The bottom image was taken from the George Street Bridge. The Reading Fairgrounds can be seen including the grandstand for the race track. The rear of Boscov's North can also be seen. Today this area is occupied by the Fairgrounds Square Mall. Both photographs Jay Leinbach.

Top: Following the RDG 3635 is Central Railroad of New Jersey diesel 2508. It was not uncommon to see foreign motive power passing through Reading. Other railroads which were seen on occassion included the Western Maryland RR, the Baltimore & Ohio RR, the Chessie System, and the Norfolk Western RR. Reading Transportation Museum.

Middle & Bottom: Conrail came about on the day these photographs of train RN15 were taken on April 1, 1976. Robert Gottschall photographed the motive power from the George Street Bridge and then ran behind the Schwambach's Diner, a favorite eating establishment of railroad crews and rail fans, to capture a friendly wave from the brakeman.

Top: In August, 1975, diesel locomotive 1501 pulls a string of Penn Central gondolas underneath the George Street Bridge at Belt Line Junction. This SW900m diesel was rebuilt from a Baldwim VO660 during the summer of 1961 and was assigned to the class SWE-4. The "SW" stood for switcher, the "E" for EMD, and the "4" meant that it was radio equipped. The engine provided numerous years of service for the Reading Railroad and Conrail.
Bottom: U30C 6304, GP39-2 3408, and GP35 3653 haul a heavy freight train through the Belt Line Junction Interlocking in October, 1975. Both photographs Jay Leinbach.

Top & Middle: Two different EMD rebuilt switchers glide through Belt Line Junction. Jay Leinbach.
Bottom: Belt Line Junction received its name from being the joining point of the Reading Belt Line with the Main Line. The freight is leaving the Belt Line. Just one-quarter mile north of this location the train will leave the main line and continue its journey on the Blandon Low Grade. RDG Transportation Museum.

Top & Middle: GP35 3623, followed by GP30 3613, passes through Belt Line Junction in 1976. Belt Line Junction was a very active place, making it a great location for rail fans. Between trains many rail fans rested on the bench awaiting the next train. Being on the far right track indicates that this train is bound for the Belt Line and will bypass the city. Jay Leinbach.

Bottom: This interesting lashup of two GP7 diesel locomotives (626 and 633) sandwiching two MP15 diesels (2777 and 2780) is pulling train RN-16 westward (north) out of the Reading Yards, through Belt Line Junction, on its way to Newberry (Williamsport) on May 22, 1976. Reading Transportation Museum.

Top: Just north of the junction of the Belt Line with the Main Line, the Blandon Low Grade jettisons eastward to Blandon and the junction with the East Penn Branch. The Blandon Low Grade was constructed to eliminate the need of extra motive power on trains climbing the Temple Grade. A portion of the Blandon Low Grade used the right-of-way of the Schuylkill & Lehigh Branch.

This image depicts an eastbound freight beginning its journey on the Blandon Low Grade on June 28, 1975. Jay Leinbach. **Middle:** The engineer's view of Belt Line Junction from the cab of diesel 2776. Robert Gottschall took this photo on February 8, 1976. **Bottom:** A perspective from the cab window of diesel 7602 as it heads north with train RN-16 through the Belt Line Junction area in March, 1976. The tracks curving off to the right are the Blandon Low Grade. Reading Transportation Museum.

Top: Three different classes of diesel locomotives pull this westbound freight train. The train will soon pass underneath the Tuckerton Road overpass, circa 1975. Jay Leinbach.

Middle: Traveling underneath the "Road to Nowhere" (currently Route 222) FP7s 903 & 902 head eastbound with a NRHS special on May 21, 1972. **Bottom:** The Reading crossed the Schuylkill River north of Tuckerton on Peacock's Lock Bridge, an impressive stone arch designed by G.A. Nicolls. This is the fireman's view of train RN crossing Peacock's Bridge in March, 1976. Both photographs Reading Transportation Museum.

Top: FP7 A units 902 and 900 with a five coach passenger train approach Leesport on May 6, 1973. Although many consider this area as West Leesport, the Reading RR referred to this location simply as Leesport. The Pennsylvania RR constructed a rail line through Leesport in 1885 and maintained a relatively large cattle pen and chutes. In direct response to this competition, the Reading Railroad spent nearly $1,000 over the next five years on facility improvements at Leesport and was able to capture approximately 50% of the Pennsylvania Railroad's business. Reading Transportation Museum. **Middle:** On occasion, freight cars will misbehave! This was the case in these two views of a derailment and subsequent pile up of freight cars in downtown Leesport in 1954. Sam Lenhart. **Bottom:** The circa 1877 Leesport Station as seen from train RN in March, 1976. Reading Transportation Museum.

Page 59: Three views of the SPENO Rail Grinding Service train at work at Dauberville on November 11, 1961. Providing the motive power is unit 532, a Baldwin AS16 diesel locomotive. Other Reading Railroad equipment in the train were cabooses 94057 and 90702 and an old steam locomotive tender. Although moved from its original location, the Dauberville Station is one of only two Main Line stations to survive in Berks County. The station was built circa 1905. Bruce Adams.

MOHRSVILLE

Top: The date is March 30, 1976, and in 36 hours the Reading Railroad would become part of Conrail and cease rail operations. EMD built GP39-2 3405 is providing the motive power for a work train in front of the Mohrsville Station. In 1976 this depot was one of the oldest surviving on the Main Line, being built circa 1864. The station had been converted into a mushroom house and was torn down in the 1980s. Reading Transportation Museum.

Middle: Two weeks before the top photograph was taken, Robert Gottschall, Jr. took this image of the Mohrsville station through the window of a diesel locomotive. The train is RN, the Reading to Newberry freight train. Reading Transportation Museum.

SHOEMAKERSVILLE

Bottom: Shoemakersville station was built circa 1877. Shoemakersville was one of the few locations within the Schuylkill River Valley where the Reading Railroad's business was second to that of the Pennsylvania Railroad. The steep road grade leading to the station and its location on the west bank of the river were the two main reasons for the Reading's inability to generate large amounts of revenue at this location. Jay Leinbach Collection.

Top: Eastbound train No. 8 makes a station stop at Hamburg on August 29, 1960. **Bottom:** A "general purpose" diesel locomotive on the Reading was the GP7 engine built by EMD. They pulled both passenger trains as depicted in the top image as well as freight trains. GP7s 602 and 607 ease into Hamburg with a local eastbound freight train on August 16, 1960. Both photographs Bruce Adams.

Page 62: A St. Clair to Reading extra freight at Hamburg in August, 1962. The man standing on the ground talking to the train crew is John Kistler, the railroad's agent at Hamburg. Diesels have both a front and a rear end. The "F" stenciled between the grab bars in the bottom image signifies that this end was the front. The front and rare of an ALCO RS3 was designated by a "1" or a "2." Note the "2" stenciled at the rare of diesel 499. Bruce Adams.

Top & Middle: The first train Bruce Adams photographed was train NH2 on July 30, 1960. The train is approximately one mile north of the Hamburg Station. Our gratitude is due to Mr. Adams for capturing many more railroad scenes on film. Fulfilling his passion for railroading, he hired onto the Pennsylvania Railroad and still works as an engineer for the Norfolk Southern Railroad out of Dillerville Yard. **Bottom:** Just north of Hamburg train No. 7 is about to duck under the Pennsylvania Railroad on its way to Pottsville on July 31, 1960. Bruce Adams.

PORT CLINTON

Top: Port Clinton was a very important junction on the Reading. The Little Schuylkill Branch, the line to Tamaqua with connections north, met the Main Line at this location. In 1873 the railroad spent $3,200 on constructing a large station. Other facilities were also constructed at Port Clinton, including an engine house. By the time this color slide of Port Clinton was taken in May, 1964, the railroad's improvements had been torn down. RDG Transportation Museum. **Middle:** A desolate view of Port Clinton from train RN in March, 1976. RDG Transportation Museum. **Bottom:** A filthy and grimy RDC rounds the curve at Port Clinton in April, 1970. Paul Carpenito.

ROBESONIA

Top: Westbound on the Lebanon Valley Branch, GP35s 3633 & 3642 haul a freight past the halfway point between Womelsdorf and Robesonia in November, 1975. Jay Leinbach. **Middle:** The North American Refractory siding is the track on the extreme right. GP30 3610 and U30C 6301 provide motive power for this westbound train. Jay Leinbach.

WOMELSDORF

SINKING SPRING

Top: On a brisk, cold day in January, 1970, GP35 3624, along with two other units, pulls a train from Rutherford to Reading. The Sinking Spring Station and freight house have been saved, moved, and restored by the Sinking Spring Historical and Heritage Park Society. It's well worth a visit. Jay Leinbach Collection.

Page 66: *Here she comes. . .There she goes.* U30C 6304 and C630 5210 with a long drag of hopper cars runs past West Lawn on their way eastward in May, 1975. The Reading RR never maintained a station in West Lawn. Passengers had to use the Wyomissing Station or the Sinking Spring Station. Reading Transportation Museum.

Top: Construction for the planned Reading to Lancaster highway has begun, requiring a new bridge to straddle the Lebanon Valley Railroad at Wyomissing to carry Penn Avenue up and over the tracks. Over twenty years after this January, 1975, image of GP39-2 3413 leading an eastbound freight, the highway was finally finished. Paul Carpenito. **Bottom:** A westbound freight, with NMO class caboose 94043 bringing up the rear, speeds past the Wyomissing highway construction site in June, 1975. Reading Transportation Museum.

LEBANON VALLEY JUNCTION

Top: Three cabooses on the rear of a freight is unusual. However, when equipment needed to be relocated to meet the needs of the railroad at other locations attaching them to a freight train was the cheapest method. It also likely that the cabooses came to Reading for repairs or inspection and are now being returned to their assigned locations. Paul Carpenito. **Middle Left:** Two GP7s 606 and 603 in pusher service on April 17, 1953. Robert Wanner. **Middle Right & Bottom:** The railroad would attach extra motive power to the rear of eastbound freight trains at Lebanon Valley Junction to assist the heavy trains to ascend the steep Temple Grade. Baldwin AS16 551 and 553 push a freight past a westbound freight being hauled by FT 256 A&B on April 10, 1953. Robert Wanner.

Page 69: Traveling along the Reading Belt Line is a freight train being hauled by engine 2112, a T-1 class locomotive. Robert Wanner was standing on the Lebanon Valley Bridge to take this April 3, 1953, photograph. Nineteen years later, from the same location, Jim Bross captured T-1 2102 pulling a special in May, 1972.

Top: Steam locomotive powered freight trains were able to stop at Lebanon Valley Junction to have their tenders filled with water. There were water plugs on the Reading Belt Line as well as on the Lebanon Valley Branch. At one time there was even a coaling tower at this location. On April 2, 1953, the fireman of locomotive 1967 watches the cistern filling with water. Robert Wanner. **Bottom:** Traveling on the Reading Belt Line, an eastbound freight crosses over Buttonwood Street. The bridge which carries the Lebanon Valley Branch over the Schuylkill River can be seen to the right of the train. Robert Wanner.

Page 71: Two views of SW900m switching diesels moving through the junction tracks. In August, 1973, diesel 1502 is on the Reading Belt Line while its sister, unit 1510, has just left the Belt Line and is making its way upgrade on the connection track to the Lebanon Valley Branch in April, 1972. Both photographs Paul Carpenito.

Top: GP 35 3635 leads an eastbound freight train down the connecting track. The train originated in Rutherford and is making its way to Philadelphia. The Lebanon Valley Junction sign can be seen to the left of the diesel's cab. This location has been renamed and is currently known as "Leisey." **Middle:** Three units pull this westward freight train in July, 1973. **Bottom:** Lebanon Valley Junction tower can be seen behind C630 5302. **Page 73:** A short but very interesting freight train hauled by GP7 608 passes the skyline of Reading in February, 1974. Paul Carpenito.

Page 74: A long string of empty hopper cars stretch behind three diesel locomotives in November, 1973. The tail end of the train is on the east side of the Tulpehocken Bridge. Note the two different style of number boards on C630 5309. The number board of the right is the style of the Reading Railroad steam locomotives. One wonders the circumstances behind why one of the number boards was replaced. Paul Carpenito.

Top: In this fall of 1974 view of switcher 1512 at Lebanon Valley Junction, the Schuylkill River looks refreshingly blue. **Bottom:** Reading's skyline can be seen behind this freight train as it travels around the city on the Reading Belt Line in early April, 1972. Both photographs Paul Carpenito.

Top: Scenes such as this were not very common in the early 1970s. First generation RS3 diesel 491 is the lead unit of a freight train on the Reading Belt Line as it approachs Lebanon Valley Junction. First generation diesels were usually placed behind the newer and more powerful second generation units. **Bottom:** This westbound freight crossing the Schuylkill River in March, 1971, on its approach to Lebanon Valley Junction, brings our exploration of one of Reading's outstanding rail fan locations to a conclusion. Both photographs Paul Carpenito.

Top & Middle: The Reading Railroad's wreck train was dispatched to clean up several hopper cars which derailed along the Lebanon Valley Branch near Schuylkill Avenue in May, 1971. SW900m diesel locomotive 1517 provided the motive power for the wreck train. The hook appears to be crane 90906, which was stationed out of Reading and operated under its own steam power. Amazingly, this steam crane survived into the early Conrail era. Reading Transportation Museum.

Bottom: The last grade crossing in Reading to be protected by a watchman was on the Lebanon Valley Branch at 3rd Street. This June 26, 1966, photograph shows that the gates had to be lowered by hand. Charles Houser

Top: By the time August 30, 1960, rolled around the once popular train, "Queen of the Valley" was reduced to one coach. The train did haul several cars of mail. An old CNJ coach with woven straw seat cushions was a regular to this train. Bruce Adams. **Middle:** Coming off of the Blandon Low Grade, a freight meets the East Penn Branch. The original route curved towards Reading to the left of the diesels. Jay Leinbach. **Bottom:** An eastbound freight has just crossed over Route 73 on July 10, 1976. The roof of the Blandon Hotel can be seen to the right of the engines. Jay Leinbach Collection.

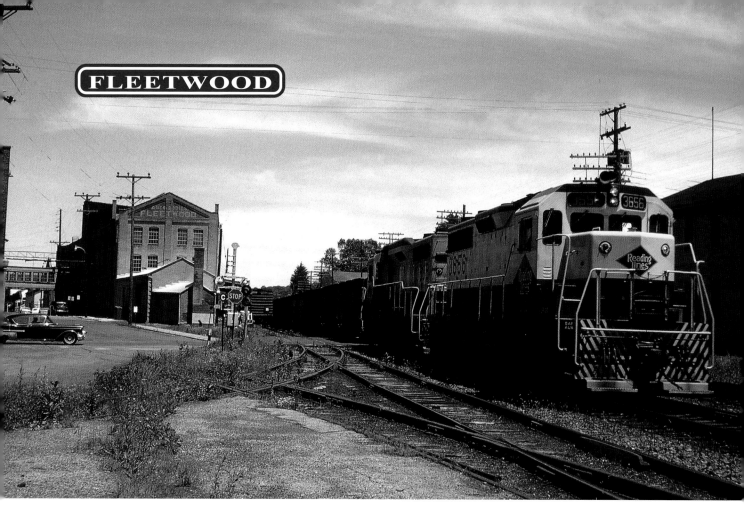

FLEETWOOD

Top: GP35 3656 leads a freight train through Fleetwood towards Reading in October, 1966. The Fleetwood Station is to the back of the photographer. Charles Houser. **Bottom:** In July 1975, a pair of U Boats with a string of C&O hopper cars at Lyons near the Deka Battery plant. Lyons was named for Mr. Evelyn Lyons, the chief engineer of the East Pennsylvania Railroad. Reading Transportation Museum.

LYONS

TOPTON

Top: A westward freight train passed the Topton Station and GP7 616 with the East Penn local in October, 1966. Topton was the highest point on the East Penn Branch and was once known as Haas' Summit. It was also the location where the Allentown Railroad met the East Penn Branch. The Allentown Railroad was chartered in 1853 to construct a line from Allentown to the P&R Main Line. Although improvements and grading were done in Allentown and at many other locations along the line, only the segment between Topton and Kuztown was constructed. Charles Houser. **Bottom:** In June 1969, an Allentown to Reading freight passes the local headed to Kutztown. The sole RS3 diesel with one box car is bound for Kutztown. Jay Leinbach Collection.

HINTERLEITER

Top: Rural scenes such as this image of GP35 3646 passing a farm along the Allentown Railroad at Hinterleiter were common on the Reading in the East Penn Valley. Jay Leinbach. **Bottom:** Two views of ALCO-built diesel locomotives servicing the railroad's customers at Kutztown. The Agway building was the former station. Reading Transportation Museum and Paul Carpenito.

KUTZTOWN

BERKLEY STATION

Page 82: Two views of switching diesel 1510 working the Schuylkill & Lehigh Branch. The top image was taken at the former Berkley Station site while the bottom view depicts the tracks at Evansville. Traffic from the Portland Cement Company kept this portion of the branch from Temple to Evansville from being torn up with the remainder of the branch in the late 1960s and early 1970s. Today the WK&S Railroad offers tourist rides on this branch between Kempton and Wanamakers. Reading Transportation Museum.

EVANSVILLE

Top: Passenger service on the Schuylkill & Lehigh Branch ceased in April, 1949, but on occassion special rail fan trips were operated over the branch. Several miles north of the Berks County line was the town of New Tripoli. A June 23, 1957, special makes a photo stop at New Tripoli, the author's boyhood town. My interest in trains began walking the abandoned right-of-way salvaging spikes, tie plates and even a brake wheel. Reading Transportation Museum.

NEW TRIPOLI

READING

Middle: The Reading Railroad operated a branch along the riverfront in Reading known as the West Reading Branch. Sections of the Pennsylvania Railroad were built parallel to that branch. During the first months of Conrail, Spring of 1976, GP7 sits in the old Pennsylvania Railroad Yard. Someone has chalked the words "Conrail / RDG" on the side of the unit. The tracks behind the unit were the West Reading Branch. Jay Leinbach. **Bottom:** Switching on the West Reading Branch. William C. Cauff, Jr.

WERTZ WAREHOUSE C

VINEMONT

Page 84: With Conrail looming, Robert Gottschall, Jr. captured the last Reading Railroad operated Reading & Columbia Branch local on March 30, 1976. MP15s 2772 and 2778 provided the motive power while class NMo caboose 94049 bought up the rear. These three images depict the train at Vinemont. Reading Transportation Museum.

Top: Preparing to leave the Reading Yards, the Joanna Turn sits in front of the Spring Street Yard Office in September, 1971. ALCO RS3s 450, 449 and two unidentified units are providing the motive power. Four RS3 diesel locomotives were regularly assinged to this heavy train. Paul Carpenito. **Bottom:** Arriving back from the Grace Mine, the Joanna Turn passes the Outer Station on May 21, 1970. Reading Transportation Museum.

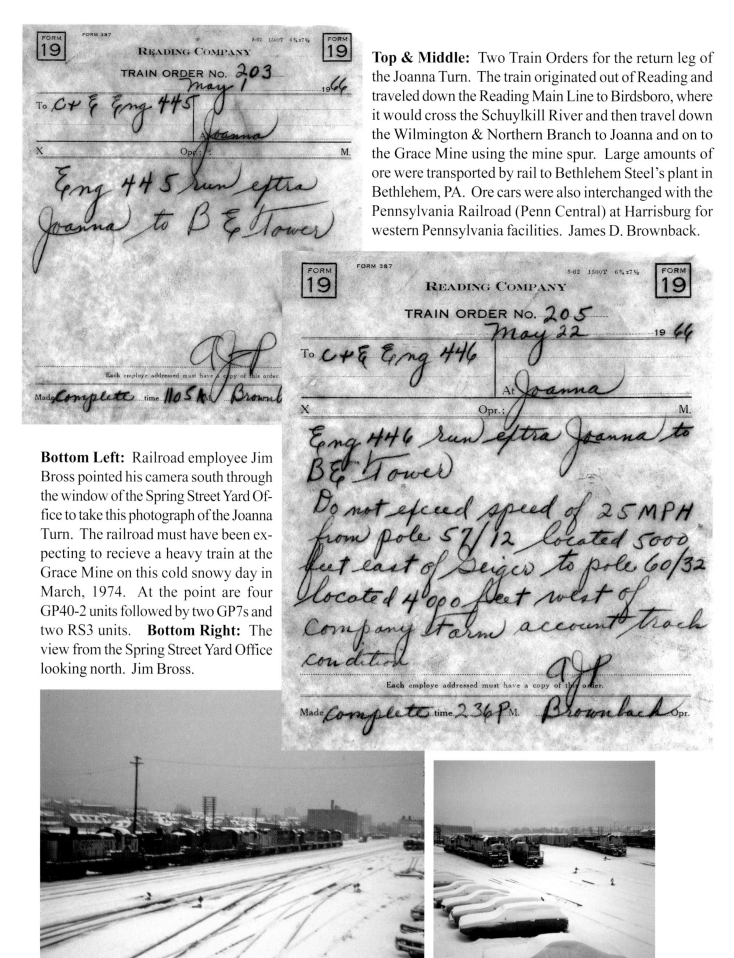

FORM 387   FORM **19**   FORM **19**   5-62 1500T 6¾x7½

READING COMPANY
TRAIN ORDER NO. 203
May 1   19 66

To C+ & Eng 445
At Joanna
X   Opr.;   M.

Eng 445 run extra
Joanna to B & Tower

Each employe addressed must have a copy of this order.

Made Complete time 1105 AM Brownb

Top & Middle: Two Train Orders for the return leg of the Joanna Turn. The train originated out of Reading and traveled down the Reading Main Line to Birdsboro, where it would cross the Schuylkill River and then travel down the Wilmington & Northern Branch to Joanna and on to the Grace Mine using the mine spur. Large amounts of ore were transported by rail to Bethlehem Steel's plant in Bethlehem, PA. Ore cars were also interchanged with the Pennsylvania Railroad (Penn Central) at Harrisburg for western Pennsylvania facilities. James D. Brownback.

FORM **19**   FORM 387   5-62 1500T 6¾x7½   FORM **19**

READING COMPANY
TRAIN ORDER NO. 205
May 22   19 66

To C+ & Eng 446
At Joanna
X   Opr.;   M.

Eng 446 run extra Joanna to B & Tower
Do not exceed speed of 25 MPH from pole 57/12 located 5000 feet east of Geiger to pole 60/32 located 4000 feet west of Company Farm account track condition

Each employe addressed must have a copy of this order.

Made Complete time 236 PM. Brownback Opr.

Bottom Left: Railroad employee Jim Bross pointed his camera south through the window of the Spring Street Yard Office to take this photograph of the Joanna Turn. The railroad must have been expecting to recieve a heavy train at the Grace Mine on this cold snowy day in March, 1974. At the point are four GP40-2 units followed by two GP7s and two RS3 units. **Bottom Right:** The view from the Spring Street Yard Office looking north. Jim Bross.

Top: Reading Company Destination Reports are valuable documents of history, for they depict what was really moving over the railroad. Station Agent James D. Brownback completed these two reports while working at Joanna. The reports not only show the number of cars leaving the Grace Mine that day but also the number of freight cars on hand and ready for usage. James D. Brownback.

Bottom: GP40-2s 3672, 3673 and 3674 return to Reading with the Joanna Turn and are crossing over Chestnut Street, and will soon pass an RDC sitting at the Franklin Street Station in November, 1974. Paul M. Carpenito.

Top Left: Engineer Bruce Adams shifting freight cars at the PRR's Pottstown Yard in August, 1966. **Top Right:** Lock was located south of Pottstown on the west side of the Schuylkill River.

Middle: Conductor P.R. Boyer gives hand signals to the engineer of Train S4 at the Pennsylvania Railroad's Pottstown Yard in August, 1966. Two ALCO diesel locomotives provide motive power.

Bottom: While waiting for permission to cross the Reading Railroad's W&N Branch in Birdsboro, Bruce Adams took this image of "Brooke" (BE) Tower. The PRR paid $8,660.66 to the Reading Railroad for the construction of the tower in 1883-84. All photographs Bruce Adams.

Top: Two views of the East Reading Pennsylvania Railroad (Penn Central) Yard in May, 1972. The yard was actually located in the current municipality of West Reading. A turntable was still maintained in the yard to turn Dana Corporation gondola cars. Jim Bross.

Middle: PC diesel 2204 heads a train underneath the Penn Street bridge and is on its way to drop off and pick up cars from Dana and Cartech in May, 1972. These two industries were the Penn Central's two largest customers in Reading. The corner of the building on the right was the original Pennsylvania Railroad Station in Reading. Conrail used the building as a freight house. Jim Bross. **Bottom:** This May, 1971, view of the Penn Central Yard along the riverfront in Reading is slightly misleading. Reading was not a major facility for the Penn Central, nor did a large amount of freight pass into or out of Reading on the PC. The nine diesel units depicted would suggest otherwise. Jim Bross.

Top: The remnants of Hurricane Agnes on June 23, 1972, greatly affected the Penn Central Railroad, formerly the Pennsylvania RR and New York Central. Their yard in Reading was nearly washed off the map. Sam Lenhart captured the devatation shortly after the storm had passsed.

Middle: Where were you on October 4, 1953? Rail fan Robert Wanner remembers that day well. On this day ran the last regularly scheduled Pennsylvania Railroad passenger train from Reading to Philadelphia occurred. Understanding the historical significance of this event, he was one of the passengers aboard the train. Mr. Wanner posed with steam locomotive 1600 at Reading before train No. 686 steamed away for the last time.   **Bottom:** The Reading Railroad's West Reading Branch paralleled the Pennsylvania Railroad along Reading's riverfront. The two railroads fiercely competed for the rail traffic in this area. Circa 1974, Reading diesel 1514 passes the PRR yard just south of Penn Street. We are into the Penn Central era. However, the Baldwin switching diesel locomotive still displays its Pennsylvania Railroad heritage. Craig Bossler.

Top: A tender from a class J1 steam locomotive was used as a diesel fueling station in Reading. Flooding caused by Hurricane Agnes contaminated the fuel with mud and water. The PC decided to scrap the tender in March, 1973. A piece of the tender was preserved by the Reading Transportation Museum.

Bottom: An NW2 class switching diesel locomotive sits inside the Penn Central Yard, formerly the Pennsylvania Railroad Yard, along the riverfront in Reading in July, 1973. The main yard stretched from Penn Street southward to Franklin Street. Paul Carpenito.

Top: Penn Central Railroad diesel locomotives 2236 and 2227 await their next assignment. The wooden building behind the engines was the Pennsylvania Railroad freight house. Years of neglect and the forces of Mother Nature have taken its toll on the building as depicted in this Decmber, 1973 view. The building was constructed in 1884. Reading Transportation Museum.

Middle & Bottom: A Baldwin Locomotive Works switching diesel locomotive performs its duties at Hamburg on August 11, 1960. The caboose, or cabin car as they were referred to on the Pennsylvania Railroad, is PRR 980807. Bruce Adams.

Top: In 1926 Brill built this trolley for the Reading Transit Company. The trolley was used in service until 1952. This image depicts the trolley at Pennwyn along the Reading to Mohnton line during the early 1950s. George Washington Gerhart photograph from the collection of John Stoudt, Jr.

Bottom: The motorman operating car 810 on the Mohnton line smiles for the camera. In all likelihood the motorman is Morris Fisher, who was a regular operator. George Washington Gerhart photograph from the collection of John Stoudt, Jr.

Top: Trolley 807 at Mohnton. This 1924 Reading Traction Co. assembled car was nearly thirty one feet long. Buses took over nearly all of the trolley lines in Reading in 1947 with the exception of the Mohnton line. The Reading Street Railway Company held a 999 year lease on the line with a $50,000 forfeiture clause in the event of the stoppage of electric trolley cars. This clause allowed the line to operate into 1952 until an agreement could be made with the heirs of Joseph and Daniel Shepp (the original owners), releasing the company from paying the forfeiture money. **Bottom:** Car 810 crossing the Wyomissing Creek in Mohnton. George Washington Gerhart from the collection of John Stoudt, Jr.

Top: These tracks are located just beyond the outfield of George Field, Reading High's baseball field. Sixth Street runs along the side of the tracks. The railroad tower in the background was known as "Water." **Bottom:** The date is January 7, 1952, a sad day for Berks County residents. Car 807, with car 806 close behind, left 5th & Penn Street for Mohnton for the last time, bringing an end to uninterrupted service since September 4, 1891. Both photographs George Washington Gerhart from the collection of John Stoudt, Jr.

Page 96: Car 307 sits in the car storage yard beside of the car barn at Tenth & Exeter Streets, Reading. In 1901 the Brill Company built this fifty two foot trolley for use on the Oley Valley line - Reading to Boyertown. The car was originally number 7. Around 1916 all seven of the 1901 Brill built Oley Valley cars were renumbered into the 300 series. The car was rebuilt as an express car circa 1917 and was rebuilt again in April, 1927, back to a passenger car. Shortly after 1940 five of the Oley Valley cars were retired. Cars 302 and 307 remained in service until early 1947. In 1947 car 307 became the personal property of J.P. Costello, General Superintendent of the Reading Street Railway Company, and he had it placed in his backyard along Gibralter Road in the Reiffton area. This car still exists located along Hopewell Road near the Berks and Chester County line. The other ex-Oley Valley car 302 was sold along with RSR car 91, and it also still exists as part of a dwelling located just outside Oley, Pennsylvania.

This is a very old and rare color image of car 307. The broadside on the front of the car reads " Italian Day - Tony Galento - Sunday, August 13, 1939 - Reading Fair Grounds." Color photographs from the 1930s are very uncommon! Less than two months before Reading's Italian day, Tony "Two-Ton" Galento knocked down heavyweight boxing champion Joe Louis in the second round. During the fourth round champion Joe Louis fought hard and won the match with a knockout. The June 28, 1939, title match was held in Yankee Stadium, New York City. William C. Cauff, Jr. Collection.